BEARDED DRAGONS FOR

BEGINNERS:

THE ULTIMATE GUIDE FOR KEEPING AND CARING FOR A

HEALTHY BEARDED DRAGON

Table of Contents

Introduction

If you've been considering having a bearded dragon as a pet, or if you've just got your first bearded dragon, then you're probably reading this because you need a bit more information about how to look after your dragon. Dragons require quite a bit more care and time than most people realize. They are a fantastic pet, full of personality and life, but like any pet, they do need to be looked after.

They need food. They need routine cleaning. And they need to be handled. If you look after your bearded dragon then you will have a wonderful pet, and companion. But, as with any animal, you must be prepared to put the effort into it.

History of the Dragon

Bearded Dragons originate from the dry semi-deserts of Central Australia. They're used to arid and rocky conditions and as a result of this love both the heat and climbing (they really love climbing). It's important to make the distinction between a desert and a semi-desert; the traditional habitat of a bearded dragon isn't bone dry. Like all animals surrounded by similar conditions, bearded dragons flock to the areas that have the most vegetation and water. Your vivarium (housing) setup should mimic those conditions.

If you're not lucky enough to live in a warm climate like Australia, you'll need to make sure that you're able to accommodate your new friend's heating needs. Bearded dragons like warmth so a heated vivarium is a must. Again this is covered in later chapters.

Exporting bearded dragons from Australia is now illegal, however this ruling was only made after hundreds of thousands had made their way to dealers around the world. Although beardies originate from Australia, you'll probably be buying yours from a local pet shop or a breeder in the next town or city.

The geographical origins of the Bearded Dragon lizard are still being intensely speculated. However, scientists tend to agree this species might originate in the central Australian desert. In present, this fascinating creature can be found in central and eastern Australia, where it is known to be a protected species, and the law is very strict. Some species (about six in number) can also be found in New Guinea.

Although the Bearded Dragon also lives in several arid, rocky regions in the United States, it remained unidentified for quite a long time. It didn't enjoy too much popularity outside Australia. But since its appearance has intrigued so many tourists and zoologists, some species were brought to zoos and continued to be regarded as unknown for a few more years.

The Pogona Bearded Dragon was first observed around 1820. Nowadays, it has become one of the most popular pets in the entire world. At first an intriguing little fellow in Australia, then unidentified in the United States... when did everything happen so fast?

Rumor has it that tourists traveling to Australia snuggled out a group of Bearded Dragons and brought them to Germany, where they had been cared for and bred. The trend of having a Pogona Dragon as a pet has become widespread ever since.

Surprisingly, we didn't know too much about the Pogona Dragon – at least not until 2005, when a group of scientists at Melbourne University discovered a pair of glands able to produce venom. There is no reason to worry though – the venom is mild and therefore harmless to people.

Prior to the discoveries at Melbourne, Frost and Etheridge developed a comprehensive assessment in 1989; a general discussion about all lizard species in the same family as the Pogona Dragon. This assessment came in response to Moody, who had been the first to provide a scientific approach to the matter 9 years earlier, in 1980. Later on, in 2000, Macey et al and Honda et al approached this topic from a genetic perspective and focused their research on mitochondrial DNA loci.

Chapter 1: Understanding the Bearded dragon

Unshaven mythical beasts are semi-arboreal (tree-abiding) and some of the time like to roost off the ground. There ought to likewise be concealing spots, for example, empty logs, for your whiskery monster to feel great.

Types of Bearded Dragon

German Bearded Dragons

These are quite different in looks and less sleek than their counterparts. Typically, sandy in color, the belly area of the dragon is larger than other breeds, also I must say that their color is amazing!

The breeders of German Bearded Dragons have managed to make the breed 50 percent larger than the average bearded dragon. Because of their larger size, these dragons often go under the name "German Giant Bearded Dragons". The color range is also of interest to breeders since unique colors can be bred.

Leatherback Bearded Dragons

As you can imagine, the back on this dragon does appear to look a little like worn leather, though the color is varied. The general overview of this breed is that the scales are smaller and this makes the dragon feel nicer to stroke with your hand.

Red Bearded Dragons

There are three types of red bearded dragons and the color depends very much upon the breeding practices. For example, the more the dragon's breed, the deeper the red color can become. Thus those bought from established breeders may all come in the darker shade of red known as Ruby Red, while younger breeds may come in the color of Blood Red which is slightly less deep in color or the standard red. There have been several varieties that have been bred using red bearded dragons bred with other colors. Thus the color range available is vast, resulting in orange, tangerine, citrus and other colors that are very attractive.

Yellow Bearded Dragons

Breeders will often cross these with other colors to produce a good range of colors anywhere between a bright yellow citrus color to orange.

Albino Dragons

These are less likely to be something you will find in a pet store, but the albino breed of bearded dragons is very attractive and sparklingly white. These give off a very delicate coloring.

Most of the dragons that you are able to buy from a breeder will be a variety of the colors shown above, but there is something else to bear in mind. Not only are there types and colors. There are also different species, which makes this reptile's appearance extremely individual and varied.

It may be worthwhile checking out the type of dragon because the looks vary so much. All species names being prefixed with Pogona, you need to understand the difference between the various species because this can affect the type of tank that you purchase, as dragons vary in full grown size. The Pogona Vitticeps grow up to 24 inches in length as opposed to the Henry Lawsoni which only grows to 12 inches.

Some breeds that you may find in encyclopedias may not be available as pets since many of the attractive species are rare and are not generally sold. It's a good idea to talk about the behavior traits of your chosen dragon with the pet store or breeder. This can, for example, tell you whether the dragon enjoys climbing or not. Information like this is valuable since it will give you ideas on what to buy to make the environment-friendly and as comfortable as possible for your dragon.

Fun Facts about Bearded Dragons

Bearded Dragons can run 15.5 kilometers or 9 miles per hour.

In the wild, bearded dragons often run on 2 legs rather than 4 when escaping predators. Although this is slower than running on 4 legs, the additional height helps them to cool down their body temperature.

Changing color is used to regulate body temperature and to disguise itself from predators in the wild. Changing to a lighter color can also help to deflect sunlight which in turn prevents the beardie from overheating – very useful when you live in the middle of a semi-desert.

Males can grow up to 24 inches in length, while females tend to grow to around 20 inches.

A bearded dragon's tail usually makes up just under half its length.

Males have larger heads than females and both have wedge-shaped heads.

Bearded dragons use their beards to make them appear larger to predators.

The Eastern Bearded Dragon used to colloquially be referred to as a Jew dragon. This wasn't meant to be racist; but simply referred to the fact that both tended to have prominent beards.

The average life expectancy of a bearded dragon is 7-10 years, however some bearded dragons live for more than this, some even up to 15 years.

Life Stages of a Bearded Dragon

Every beardie will go through four life stages (excluding the time within the egg).

Stage 1: The Hatchling

The characteristics that match this period are strong growth spurts and a change in eating habits (bearded dragons have big appetites when they're younger, especially for insects). At this stage, a bearded dragon will be anywhere between 2 and 8 inches in length at which point it will move onto the next stage of the life cycle.

Stage 2: Juvenile

The period in which bearded dragons are referred to as juveniles usually lasts from the first 3-6 months of their life. At this stage they could be up to 12 inches in length and may weigh up to 200-250 grams.

Stage 3: Sub-Adults

The sexual-maturity years. If that sounds like an Adrian Mole book, it isn't, although it will certainly feel like it for you. Having just reached this phase of their lives, it may feel like there's suddenly only one thing on their minds, the males at least. However although beardies can breed at this stage, since they're still growing, many breeding experts recommend not allowing them to do so just yet. Sub-adults will be around 6-18 months in age, weigh between 200 and 400 grams and will be roughly 13-18 inches in length.

Stage 4: Adults

18 months onwards is typically classed as adulthood and at this stage beardies are definitely able to breed. A healthy bearded dragon should weigh between 400 and 600 grams and will be roughly 18-22 inches in length.

Behavior

Unlike most reptiles, Bearded Dragons aren't short tempered. Blood thirst isn't one of their characteristics; they love to be handled and are very affectionate. All species have their own behavioral characteristics and ways to interact. None of them should take you by surprise. Here's what you have to expect…

Diurnal creatures

As we already know, Bearded Dragons are active during the day and sleep at night. Unlike other pets, it will be even more peaceful and quiet at night, so you won't have to worry about it as long as you turn the heat source off. Cats, for example will most probably wake you up while chasing and hunting insects in the dark.

Selecting your Dragon

It is highly recommended that you purchase your Dragon from reputable breeders. Make sure you are offered a health guarantee. Trustworthy breeders usually offer a six-week health guarantee. Trustworthy reptile pet stores do business with reputable breeders, and that's why it's better to get your Dragon straight from the source. Make sure the pet store provides proper care, food and hygiene to all exhibited Dragons.

It would be best to select a young, healthy Dragon. As a pet owner, it's a real pleasure to watch your fellow grow and learn new things. If you go for an older one, you can't know much about its history, skills and habits. It will be harder to teach him new habits and make him forget about the old ones. Moreover, Dragons live between five and eight years, and you will definitely want to spend as much time as possible with your new reptile friend.

However, a Dragon that is TOO young isn't an easy option either. Hatchlings are extremely hard to care for, and they might get ill or even die if the smallest mistake is made. A Dragon is perfect for adoption between two months and one or two years of age. If the previous owner or merchant doesn't know the exact age, you can perform body measurements in order to figure out yourself. A two-month-old Dragon measures about six inches in length.

When it comes to selecting your Dragon, there are also a few "good signs" and "bad signs" you should be able to notice right on the spot.

Good signs include:

You Dragon keeps its head up, just like a smug little fellow.

All toes and tail nips are in good place.

The tail base is thicker.

Healthy eyes – no mucus should be present. Eyes should be wide open and clear.

Curled up tail (towards the head).

Bad signs include:

The Dragon is lethargic and looks as if something drained its energy.

Toes and tail nips are missing.

The Dragon can barely move (because of laziness or an injury... laziness isn't a good sign at all!).

Fecal smearing is observed around vent.

Setup & Ongoing Costs

Although there are a few large initial costs such as the purchase of the vivarium, the ongoing costs of keeping a bearded dragon are relatively low.

The initial bearded dragon setup (vivarium, lighting, decorations etc can be quite expensive) but once you're set up the only real cost is food, electricity to run the light and heating. You may also need to change your bulb every year or so.

In comparison to keeping a dog or most other pets, this works out very well in the long-run, especially considering bearded dragons tend to live for 7-10 years on average.

Chapter 2: Housing the bearded dragon

Items for your Dragons Home

There are different styles of Vivarium/Terrarium but the most common are:

Wood Wooden or chipboard generally have a set of sliding glass doors and ventilation grills or mesh in the back of the unit.

Glass These units with mesh tops are generally the choice of most owners as they are the most attractive, better for viewing your dragon and easier to clean which is a major plus when it comes to the care of your pet.

As with the wooden style, dimensions can be made to suit your dragon or dragons needs. I will go into dimensions a little later.

Your dragons' home should have a *Desert, Arid Land* set up. This in simple terms just means that your dragon prefers hot and dry temperatures and thrives in desert or savanna terraria, but should also consist of a cooler area with a hide/cave so that your dragon can cool down and relax and hide away when it needs to.

Outdoors If you live in an area which is arid and warm, your dragon will thrive in outdoor cages, certainly for the summer periods.

Dimensions The minimum size home for a single dragon should be:3 feet (90cm) length x 1.5 feet (45cm) height and width.

Substrates Despite differing views to the contrary, I have used smooth (**not** sharp silica) sand as an excellent substrate for many years. The concern is about intestinal impaction, but I have never had a problem. There are other substrates like Astroturf and others which you may wish to discuss with your local pet shop or breeder.

Rocks or stone features are important for basking/viewing areas (set up under the basking light) and a stone feature can be purchased or made as a hideaway/cave.

Basking Lamp Very important for your dragon so that it may maintainits' optimum body temperature. Also purchase a timer for the lamp as you must be able to replicate daylight hours. These lamps must be controlled by a Dimming Thermostat as well as a Timer unless you are going to manually turn them down or off during the evening hours. Your dragon and you must be protected from contact with the lamp.

Ceramic Heaters and Infrared Bulbs These can produce very hot basking areas but produce no light and as with the basking lamp, they must be thermostatically controlled. Your dragon and you must be protected from contact with them.

Heat Pads & Thermostat. Heat pads or heat mats as they are sometimes known as, can be placed under the substrate. Care must be taken so that your dragon cannot dig and scratch away at the face of the heat pad. Check with the manufacturer of this item, as sometimes, if you have a glass terrarium they may suggest placing the pad/mat under the terrarium itself. The thermostat is very important, once again to regulate the temperature and to replicate day/night time temperature.

Strip Lighting Full spectrum fluorescent strip lighting is very important. These lights provide your dragon with UVA & UVB ultraviolet light with minimal heat. Ultraviolet lights promote the natural synthesis of the vitamin D3 in your dragon it also enables it to absorb calcium. There is a very complex interaction between D3 and the calcium process which is too complicated to go into in this book.

These lamps need to be on for approximately 12 - 16 hours in the summer months and dropping to 8 - 10 hours in the winter months. Most manufacturers recommend changing these lights every 9 - 12 months. Although they are still working, light wise, the UVA & UVB light diminishes over time.

Water Dish For one dragon you only require a small water dish. The water is obviously for drinking, but also helps with the humidity. Do not put too big a dish into their home as you do not want your dragon to bathe in it.

Cage Furniture Besides the rock and cave formations you can obtain propriety half logs or branches. You can also introduce potted arid land plants including dried grasses.

Thermometer and Hygrometer Quite often overlooked but two very important items for the wellbeing of your dragon as these two items allow you to monitor temperature and humidity within the terrarium.

Mist Spray Bottle. Some dragons prefer to drink from water droplets that will form on the side of the terrarium after you have sprayed inside it. A few baby dragons initially will have to learn to drink and they will not use the water dish.

Sealant You can use Aquarium Sealant if you are making your own rock/cave formations or any other features in your dragons' home, but you must make absolutely sure that the sealant has had sufficient *curing* time as per the manufacturer instructions before placing any item and certainly your dragon into the terrarium.

Small Ventilation Fan This is an optional product and most owners do not install one.

Before going into technical information about tanks, lights, heaters etc. I would advise new owners to have all of this explained when they buy the tank. It's a lot of information to take in at a time when you may be overly excited about having a new pet. If you are able to get a professional to help you to set up the tank, it will save you a lot of time and energy since you won't have to deal with any problems. A reliable seller should be able to advise you on all that is needed to set up the tank in a bearded dragon friendly way.

Baby Tank Size 20 gallon

Just like you feel comfortable in your own home, your bearded dragon also needs to feel at home and there are some pretty amazing reptile backgrounds that you can buy for your tank. These look like the desert environment in which your bearded dragon would feel right at home. These, if you buy good quality, are tear resistant. You do not need to worry about this since you can buy the exact size your tank needs and then simply tape it on the outside of the tank against a wall, so it's unlikely to cause any damage or problems.

When you have a baby dragon, you tend to use a smaller sized tank. That way you can be sure that your bearded dragon is able to locate his food. However, if you always feed by hand, then having a larger tank is not a problem. You also need to observe the baby and ensure that the food you are giving the baby is small enough for the bearded dragon to eat. Thus, it's up to you whether you want to start with a tank this small.

12-16 inch Tank Size 40 gallon

Although you can trade upward and get a larger tank later, I found that my baby bearded dragon was happier in a larger tank, provided that there was enough of interest in the tank. A place where the dragon could bask safely also seemed to affect my dragon's mood. This can be created by the use of suitable rocks, especially if you know that your bearded dragon loves to climb.

17-20 inch Tank size 50-75 gallon

At this age, your bearded dragon needs to move around and a small tank prohibits this. A 50-gallon tank can be okay for a fully grown bearded dragon unless your dragon is bigger than 20 inches if so, you should opt for the 75-gallon tank.

Keeping the bearded dragon warm

It may not be something that you have considered, though avoid gimmicks like heated rocks or any kind of heating that comes from beneath the dragon. The reason for this is that the body of the bearded dragon is very fragile and heat should not be allowed to burn the skin.

I have two thermometers in my bearded dragon's tank because you need to remember that different temperatures in the tank are needed at all times. For example, on one side of the tank, the temperature that is ideal is around 100 degrees Fahrenheit (38 °C), while the cooler side of the tank is normalized around 84 degrees Fahrenheit (29 °C).

Appropriate temperatures in the tank are critical. Similarly as with different reptiles, a temperature slope ought to be accommodated your unshaven mythical serpent, just as a lolling spot. The angle should go from 80 to 85 degrees Fahrenheit on the cool side, up to a relaxing temperature of around 95 to 105 degrees Fahrenheit. Evening time temperatures can tumble to roughly 65 to 70 degrees Fahrenheit.

Warmth can be given by means of a radiant light, fired warmer, or a mercury fume bulb in a vault reflector hood. You may have to try different things with wattage and distance from the tank to give proper temperatures.

Use thermometers in the tank to screen the temperatures at the relaxing spot, just as at one or the flip side of the warm inclination. Never depend on evaluations. In the event that important, an under-tank radiator can be utilized to enhance the warmth, particularly around evening time if the room temperature is low.

Lighting

Bearded Dragons are diurnal creatures, meaning they are active during the day, just like humans. This means you can't afford to leave the lamp on during the light – would you like it if you were forced to sleep with your lights turned on? Not turning off the lights will negatively impact your Dragon's mood and development, just like prolonged nights in front of books or computers ultimately end up damaging our vision and making us grumpy or short-tempered.

If turning the lights off at night is a must, things get a bit tricky when it comes to heating. Leaving heating devices on is not recommended, but we also know heating plays an important part in digestion. The best compromise is to feed your Dragon earlier in the day, so the digestion process will end until bedtime.

In natural habitats, temperature usually drops at night, so you don't have to worry about keeping the tank really warm at all times. Your house already provides a good night temperature, so you won't need any additional cooling devices.

Openness to UV lighting is critical for pet unshaven mythical beasts. Exceptional bright light bulbs can be found at pet stores that give UV light. Your unshaven winged serpent ought to have the option to get inside 12 creeps of these lights to profit by the UV discharged, contingent upon the kind of bulb. Follow the producer's proposals. Also, the lights ought to be coordinated through a screen top as opposed to glass, as glass sift through some UV beams.

Keep a steady day-night cycle by giving around 12 hours of light and 12 hours of dimness every day. Putting the lights on a clock can be useful.

Openness to daylight can likewise be advantageous. In the event that time outside is given, shade and asylum should be accessible, so your unshaven mythical serpent can thermo regulate. Never place your pet outside in a glass tank, as overheating will rapidly happen in the daylight.

Mugginess

Whiskery mythical beasts incline toward a mugginess level of around 35% to 40%. This emulates their common bone-dry climate. Normally this level is simply hard to keep up in the event that you live in a high-mugginess zone.

Low Humidity

What you are trying to emulate is the atmosphere that would be present in the natural habitat of the bearded dragon. Thus light and humidity should be perfect. A bearded dragon is going to need that strong light for up to 14 hours each day. The light should be defused over the whole area of the tank and you will find that most pet stores show you how the lighting systems achieve that. Furthermore, the bearded dragon needs to actually get as close as possible to the lamp for the required heat. A safe distance is up to 6 inches (15 cm) away, so when you set out your tank, you need to be able to add things like branches or rocks to help the bearded dragon to gain access higher up in the tank.

One important thing to think about when setting up the tank is that it must have a stable base and be set up near a power outlet. If you don't get the light right, your dragon can become seriously ill and thus, it's important not just to have light in the tank but to provide the amount of UVA and UVB needed.

The basking bulb also needs to be fitted, so make sure you make allowance for this when setting the tank up. For the basking bulb, do make sure that you buy your supplies from reptile experts because then you know that you are getting the right equipment.

Since bearded dragons need a low humidity environment, having a humidity meter is a must. The idea of having a screen top as opposed to a solid one is to allow the passage of air and this should cause no humidity at all. However, that really depends upon the environment in which you live, so you should position your tank where lower readings of humidity are obtained.

Basking Platform

In the warmer side of your tank, you will need a basking platform of some kind and although natural branches can be used you need to a bit wary about what type of wood you use since it can have splinters. It's better to buy a readymade one because you know that it is made of safe materials that will not harm your bearded dragon. Before buying one, you need to measure the space in the tank so that you can place it sufficiently for the dragon to bask at about 6-8 inches away from the heat lamp.

These come in the form of a bridge or rocks and your pet supply shop will be able to help you choose based on the size of your tank and your envisioned set up.

Substrate

Substrate is the material you put on the floor of your unshaven winged serpent's nook. It assists with keeping up dampness in the climate, and it can give the tank a more regular look and feel.

For adolescents, free substrate, for example, sand, ought to be dodged. There is too extraordinary a danger of ingestion either coincidentally or to clear something up, and this can prompt intestinal impaction. Paper towels or reptile floor covering can be utilized all things being equal.

For grown-ups, washed play sand (not fine silica sand) can be utilized; however paper towels or reptile cover turns out great, as well. Try not to utilize wood shavings, corn cob, pecan shell, or different substrates that could cause issues whenever gulped. On the off chance that sand is utilized, excrement can be scooped out with a feline litter scoop. Sand permits whiskery mythical beasts to burrow and tunnel, which they appreciate.

The term Substrate is defined as being the surface or material on which an organism lives, grows or obtains its nourishment. In terms of bearded dragon care the substrate is what you choose to line your bearded dragon's vivarium. There are multiple different substrates available to use in your vivarium.

Newspaper and Paper Towels

Both newspaper and paper towels are easily obtained and inexpensive. They make for good flooring if your bearded dragon has an injury (for example a severed 'quick') as they are smooth and do not have any potentially harmful edges. However there is the potential for harmful inks to be present within the paper which make them not ideal for long term use.

Artificial Grass

There are many grades of artificial grass which allows you to choose which best suits your lizard's needs. Artificial grass is widely available in hardware stores and ironically the cheapest is normally the best when it comes to lining a vivarium. The cheapest artificial grass tends to be the most flexible which makes it easier to clean as well as cheaper to replace. If artificial grass is used it is best practice to have multiple pieces cut to fit the floor of the vivarium. This allows for you to rotate the flooring when needed to clean and dry the other pieces.

Wood Chippings

Wood chippings are not considered best practice for lining a bearded dragon's vivarium but due to their popularity we have included a section on them. Wood chippings should be avoided for juvenile bearded dragons due to the fact that smaller lizards may have trouble digesting them. If you want to use wood chippings however we recommend using aspen or beech chips. Aspen shavings are decent for lining the floor of your vivarium. A great bonus is that they collect urine and faeces and can easily be scooped out with a dog or cat litter scoop. Aspen shaving only have one flaw and that is that they have to be replaced once they become dirty. However this flaw is inconsequential due to the shavings' relatively low price. Beech chippings are cheap and readily available from all reptile stores. They are not as absorbent as Aspen shavings and likewise need to be removed once they are dirtied. However they come in three different grades – small, medium and large. This allows you to choose which grade best suits your bearded dragon. It is important to note that wood chippings are normally chosen for aesthetic reasons rather than functional reasons.

Oatbran and Wheatbran

Although it sounds like a strange choice to line a vivarium both oatbran and wheatbran are great and inexpensive choices. They a very similar aesthetic as wood chippings but have the benefit of being digestible and dramatically cheaper.

Substrates to Avoid

The following substrates should be avoided due to the fact that they are either toxic or indigestible: cedar shavings, gravel, kitty litter, pesticides and fertilizer.

A hiding place for your bearded dragon

It is important when you own any animal that the animal feels safe in the environment in which he is placed. Thus, with reptiles, it's vital to have a place where the bearded dragon can hide if he wants to feel safe. When you consider the noise in an average home, there may be noises that will make your bearded dragon feel uncomfortable. Provided that you give it the space to get away from this and feel safe, then you are providing what the bearded dragon needs.

This is also needed for periods of hibernation or "brumation" when your bearded dragon has to be asleep for periods in excess of a couple of weeks.

Water container

You will also need a water container, though this should be very shallow so that your bearded dragon cannot drown. Although they generally take moisture from the greenery that you give them, having this means that your pet is never without water if this is needed.

Important Note about cleanliness

Your bearded dragon will need to have water in his tank. However, you must make sure that this is changed regularly and that there are no feces left in the water. You will be misting your dragon regularly and this will supply a lot of the moisture that is required by a bearded dragon, but, as mentioned previously, the tank should always have a shallow container of water in it to help moisture levels and to ensure that the bearded dragon has water available at all times.

Heating

A proper basking temperature is vital to a healthy digestion. Since they originate in the arid areas of Australia, they need to be kept warm. However, the temperature doesn't have to be too high either. Bearded Dragons need a cooler place to retreat and regulate their body temperature. This is why the tank must be equipped with a heating and ventilation source. Again, do NOT use hot rocks as your Dragon might suffer severe burns... unfortunately, Beardies can't tell if the rock is on or off – too hot or safe to touch. Accidents? Not on the list.

Ideal daytime temperature: 80-85 F

Ideal basking temperature: 85-110 F

Ideal night temperature: 60-70 F

As you might have probably realized by now, you can't rely on a heating lamp only. Since temperature is so important, you will need a thermostat to monitor and control the tank environment.

Chapter 3: Daily Care for Bearded dragon

Infrequently you will need to get your beardie. You might need to take him out of his pen with the goal that you can clean it, or you might need to set him up for transportation to the veterinarian. It might be that you simply need to visit with him and become acquainted with him.

Here are some do's and don'ts for taking care of your beardies:

- Try not to make sudden gets for the beardie.
- Try not to get him by his tail or any of his appendages.

- Do approach gradually and tenderly, with no undermining motions.
- Do place your finger under the jaw and expand it under the body. A child beardie will clutch your finger.
- Do transport babies by grabbing the roost they are lying on.
- Do completely bolster the beardie in the palm of the hand, tail along your lower arm, with its head confronting far from you.
- Try not to crush or push on any part of the beardie's body. Youngsters must be directed therefore, forewarned and taught how to legitimately handle the creature.
- Don't abruptly get him with a clench hand if your beardie tries to run or begins becoming eager. Rather, keep the palm of one hand level and the other one marginally measured.
- Do permit your beardie to step by step roost on your midsection or shoulder, keeping one hand relentless and prepared to bolster him. Grown-ups tend not to hang on as firmly as adolescents and infants do.
- Try not to set your beardie anyplace high off of the ground. In the event that he bounced from too high up, he could harm himself, bringing about broken appendages or toes.
- Do entice your beardies into offering so as to come to you them their most loved nourishments or treats from your hands.

- Try not to pursue your beardie around his enclosure on the off chance that he tries to escape you getting him. In the event that there is a pursuit each time you reach into handle him, he'll soon come to see your hand as an unnerving risk.
- Do be persistent. It requires investment for your beardie to become used to you, to become acquainted with you and to get the chance to trust you. Quiet, tender taking care of is best.

Getting Enough Exercise

You'll need to take some consideration in giving your beardie exercise. He's not care for a pooch that can go for a run around the square with you. One type of activity regularly utilized by zoos is called natural improvement. This keeps the hostage creatures rationally ready and physically dynamic. You put their most loved sustenance's and treats in shrouded places about the enclosure, and they move around, chase and sniff them out so as to discover them. Until your beardie gets used to this action, put two or three his treats directly before him. He'll get the thought as he watches you. Place whatever is left of the treats in easyto—find areas, and after that after he enhances, place them in trickier areas. This will show him that he gets a prize for moving around.

Cleaning

One of the chores of owning a beardie is cleaning his vivarium. This needs to be done regularly and carefully to ensure that bacteria doesn't grow.

To save yourself time in the future, make sure the vivarium is easy to clean. Glass or smooth surfaces are generally easier to clean than wood and tend to dry quickly. You should also be cleaning rocks and furniture within the vivarium, as it's possible bacteria could have started to grow on these.

You should clean the vivarium with a solution of 1:10 dilution of household bleach and water. Some people like to make a spray bottle with the solution as this ensures they are able to cover every part of the vivarium before letting it to sit. Once covered in the spray, you should leave it to sit for around 15 minutes. Rinse until you can no longer smell any bleach and then dry thoroughly with a piece of kitchen paper.

Note: You can get a pre-made reptile cleaning disinfectant from most pet stores; however the above water/bleach solution tends to work well and it is cheaper to make up.

On a daily basis it's recommended that you remove any uneaten food and any obvious faeces. The smell can quickly become overpowering and after a while you'll find yourself instinctively cleaning up faeces as soon as you see them.

Baby bearded tend to excrete around 2-3 times per day and many bearded dragon owners use kitchen towel during the first few months as it's quick and easy to replace.

You should also ensure that you have good substrate within the vivarium. Substrate is what lines the bottom of your lizard's vivarium. This should be changed on a weekly or bi-weekly basis.

Ideally your substrate should be: absorbent, digestible, easy to pick up when cleaning and should look natural both to you and your bearded dragon. Being digestible doesn't necessarily mean that your bearded dragon should be eating the substrate, it's just a fact of life that he occasionally will.

Brumation

Brumation is the term used to describe the hibernation cycle of bearded dragons. This is a response to a change in lighting or temperatures, particularly in winter or fall. Some owners adjust the setting in the vivarium to prevent brumation, but this isn't always a good idea. Brumating is part of the natural cycle of bearded dragons, and your bearded dragon should be allowed to brumate as he chooses.

How your dragon brumates depends on him. Some dragons brumate for a few days or a week, while others brumate for a few months. Some dragons nap during brumation, with period of wakefulness, others stay asleep for the whole of the brumation period.

When your dragon is brumating, he won't be as active, and he will sleep for longer periods, or he will sleep all the time. His appetite may have reduced, or he won't eat at all. A healthy dragon won't lose any weight while he is brumating, even if he eats much less than normal or doesn't eat anything. If your bearded dragon loses weight during his brumation, then he may have parasites. You should send a fecal sample for parasite testing when your think your dragon is about to start to brumate. Some owners weight their bearded dragons before they start brumating, and when they come out of brumation to record any weight changes. This is only necessary if you think your dragon might have parasites, but you might find it interesting or beneficial to keep a record of your dragon's weight.

This is not really a turmoil or an ailment. Brumation is the whiskery mythical serpent form of hibernation, however it varies in that it is set apart by occasional arousing and the transitory resumption of action and encouraging. Hibernation is one long stretch of idleness where a few reptiles go underground to get away from the compelling frosty of the winter months. A few raisers instigate brumation in their unshaven mythical beasts since they trust it helps them to get ready for the rearing season ahead.

On the off chance that your beardie does not actually brumate, there is , there is no motivation to constrain it to do as such, and children more youthful than one year ought to never be constrained. This is a prime time of development and improvement for them that ought not be interfered.

On the off chance that your beardie does brumate, here is the thing that you can do to keep him solid:

Keep the luxuriating light on 8 to 10 hours a day.

Reduce the encompassing confine temperature to 65 to 70 degrees Fahrenheit.

Provide a luxuriating place at the ordinary temperature, since a bromating beardie might choose to eat yet won't have the capacity to process without the warmth.

Continue to offer nourishment amid this period, since you never know when a bromating beardie might choose to wake up and need a supper.

Some people turn the vivarium lights off, and stop feeding the dragon until the end of brumation. However, as every dragon is very different, you should continue to keep the lights on the normal cycle throughout brumation, and continue to offer food and his regular diet. Many dragons will wake up during brumation to eat and bask occasionally. Leave some fresh vegetables in the food bowl , and watch to see if any has been eaten. You shouldn't, however, wake your dragon to bath or eat, as this can extend the brumation cycle.

As winter occurs naturally outside, many bearded dragon owners recommend that you mimic this occurrence within the bearded dragon's vivarium.

During this period (usually around 4-6 weeks although it can last for as much as 3 months) you should aim to reduce temperatures to around 24 degrees C to 27 degrees C (75 degrees F to 80 degrees F) under the basking light and the night time temperature to 16 degrees C (60 degrees F).

His appetite will reduce and he may even appear sluggish; this is completely natural – he is after all, in a natural state of rest. With a reduced appetite you won't need to feed him as much or as often – again it will appear obvious as to when he has had enough as he will simply stop eating.

Make sure the vivarium contains plenty of private areas to shelter such as hollow logs and artificial caves.

During this time you should continue to bathe your bearded dragon, although within the brumation period once every 1-2 weeks should be enough. This will help to prevent dehydration and to ensure continued cleanliness.

Handling

It's likely that once you get to know your beardie (and he gets to know you) you'll want to take him out of the vivarium to play with him. There are a few best practices to consider in order to ensure that he is properly treated and you reduce the risk of any disease spreading.

Be sure to wash your hands before and after handling your bearded dragon as beardies can harbour salmonella. You could also have bacteria or germs on your hands. Giving them a quick wash before handling reduces the chances of either you or your bearded dragon coming into contact with a disease. Hand sanitizing cream should work fine for this but remember to rinse your hands thoroughly to remove any traces from your skin.

When picking up your dragon, be sure to do so in a very gentle manner. You should hold the bearded dragon in the palm of one hand, with the other hand used to firmly stop them from trying to escape or jump off.

Bearded dragons are climbers and so they may be tempted to jump onto something else nearby. For this reason, you shouldn't hold them too high off the ground, in case their jump isn't successful.

You should **never** pick your dragon up by its tail. If you are trying to lift your bearded dragon and it is resisting, leave it be. Otherwise you risk stressing it out.

It is generally recommended that you avoid over-handling your bearded dragon in the first few weeks after he is brought home. This is especially true of juvenile or younger bearded dragons who have a tendency to get stressed if they are over-handled, particularly when adjusting to their new surroundings.

Be gentle when handling your dragon and avoid sudden hand movements. If your bearded dragon becomes defensive or nervous, you should avoid trying to pick it up. Especially avoid any swooping movements as this is the movement bearded dragons will naturally try to hide from. If possible scoop him up rather instead – a simple way to remember this is: scoop, don't swoop!

Occasionally handling your dragon during feeding time can help to disassociate you from any perceived threats.

You may have spent a lot of time and money on a bearded dragon's cage, but that does not mean that you can handle a dragon any way you like. If you mishandle a bearded dragon it won't trust you, and this makes acclimatization more difficult. Here are some general tips for safely handling bearded dragons:

1. Always approach your bearded dragon with care. Avoid startling the reptile just before picking it up. A startled bearded dragon will most likely dart to the nearest cover and, trust me it's doubly hard to handle a dragon when it's frightened.

2. Hold the dragon under its belly, and gently lift the animal from its cage. Support its entire length whenever you want to pick up the reptile.

3. Avoid hugging the reptile, or gripping its tail, or any part of its body, tightly. Instead, let the reptile rest on your hand or arm, and just let it explore its surroundings. Be very alert for minute changes in the reptile's body language; a curious dragon may suddenly feel the urge to explore the surroundings.

4. Like other pet reptiles, you can let your reptile wander in an outdoor enclosure. Just make sure that you watch it, even if you have a fine wire fence covering the area.

If your bearded dragon is a baby, then it might not be used being handled. Even some adult dragons may not be used to being handled. You can build up a relationship and trust with your dragon by hand feeding him. You can pick your dragon up. Slowly move your hands towards him, and try not to make any sudden moves that could spook him. Approach him within his field of vision, and not from the top. Dragons have a sense on the top of their heads that can pick up shadows and movement.

Slide your hand under the belly, and lift your dragon gently. Let his tail lie along your forearm and keep the dragon close to your body. If you have a baby dragon, keep one finger under his chin. He'll hold your finger for extra security. If he tries to move or run away, let him. Don't hold him tight or squeeze him, but also don't let him fall.

If you have a baby dragon, he might become a little scared or nervous. Cup one hand over him, so he has somewhere to hide and see if he calms down. You could also try offering some food. It will help your dragon associate being handled with something good.

You should never lift your dragon by his tail or limbs, and you shouldn't grab him suddenly. Don't let him fall, or put him somewhere he could fall from. Don't leave him alone in the room, and don't leave children alone with him.

You should make sure to wash your hands with an antibacterial soap after handling your dragon, and never eat or put your hands in your mouth while holding him. If you have been scratched by your bearded dragon's claws, make sure that you disinfect the scratch. If he has bitten you, disinfect the wound well, and if it gets red, or sore, see your doctor. Although, it should be noted that it is rare for bearded dragons to bite people like this.

Bathing

Bathing a bearded dragon is important for proper hygiene and to help hydrate the bearded dragon, and it should be taken once or twice a week, depending on the pet's needs. The water must be warm (about 36°C / 96.8°F) and not deep. It is enough water if it reaches the lizard's knees (for young pets) or shoulders (for adults), which means between 1.2 and 2.5 cm (0.5-1 inch).

Soap or shampoos are not recommended, as the dragon might also drink some of the bath water. The pet should stay in the water between 15 and 30 minutes, time in which water temperature should be kept at the correct value.

Some owners bathe their pet beardie in the sink or the bathtub, but for hygiene purposes, we do not recommend this. A plastic container kept only for the dragon would be more suitable. The container must be big enough to allow the pet to move. A rock or a towel can be added to give the dragon an alternative if it wants to get out from the water.

The dragon should be well dried before going back into the tank. Some dragons enjoy bathing. You run a shallow bath of lukewarm water and gently set your bearded dragon in. Some dragons like to paddle in the water, others like to drink it, and some dragons don't like it at all. Your dragon will let you know if he enjoys it or not,

Roaming your House

Once your bearded dragon is settled with you, and you can handle him. You can let him run along the floor, as long as it is clean, dry and chemical free. They might find some surfaces difficult to run on, and this can be distressing for them, but if your floor has a non slip flooring that your dragon can run on, then he can. Do not leave him unattended while he is out of his vivarium. He might decide to hide, and a lot of dragons seem to particularly like the electrical sockets in the room. Also, may dragons seem to prefer to toilet when they are out of the vivarium, so watch for any feces.

Roaming Outside

As long as you have not treated any grass or ground with any type of chemicals, then many owners report that their dragons like to get outside every once in a while. If ou take your dragon outside, never leave him unattended, and make sure he doesn't eat anything outside. Some dragons don't like to be outside, or don't like to be outside for very long. Your dragon will show you if he enjoys being outside or not. Some dragons like to look at the outside while being held, and others might like to sit in the doorway, as long as you watch your dragon, and he can't fall then he can enjoy all the views of outside, from the safety of your home.

During the hot season, keeping the bearded dragons outdoors can be a good option for their health, as they can have access to natural sunlight and high levels of ultraviolet light. The minimum temperature required for taking the pet outside is 24°C (75°F) and the owner must make sure that the lizard has full access to the sunlight.

Specialists recommend creating an outdoor habitat that is safe, keeps out predators and doesn't allow the reptile to escape. The enclosure must fulfill all the same conditions provided indoors (clean and safe floor, appropriate substrate, sanitized branches and rocks) and also to be adapted to the new environment. It should not be made of glass as this might overheat the tank. It must not be placed directly in the sunlight, but in a zone that will allow the pet to regulate his body temperature by moving from the hot area to a cooler one. Inside the enclosure, there should be at least one shelter, which can also help to prevent overheating, and multiple basking areas that can get sun throughout the day.

In the outdoor enclosure, the pet must have access to food and fresh water. During its staying outside, the bearded dragon should regularly be checked on to prevent it from being too hot or too cold. Thermometers must be used to measure temperature in the cage and on the basking spots. It is not recommended for the pet bearded dragon to remain outside during night time.

Skin Shedding

Like most reptiles, hairy mythical serpents will shed their skin all the time. It's an ordinary process and not a reason for concern, in spite of the fact that you ought to watch out for your beardie to ensure nothing turns out badly. This procedure disposes of the old skin and uncovers new underneath it, and when youthful, beardies will shed more frequently than grown-ups. Children might shed like clockwork or so whilst full—grown beardies will just do as such once, twice or three times each year.

Around a week or two preceding shedding, look for an expansion in longing in your beardie. It will drop off again amid shedding, and numerous beardies will likewise get to some degree testy and peevish.

Reptiles often shed their skin. Baby and juveniles shed their skin as they grow, so they have frequent shedding. Adults might only shed once or maybe twice a year.

Just before your dragon starts to shed, their color will become duller, and their eyes might seem a little puffed out. This isn't anything to worry about, as these are normal signs of a healthy shed.

As your dragon sheds you need to make sure that he is both clean and hydrated. You can bathe him in lukewarm water, and occasionally mist him with a spray bottle of water. The spray will help keep the skin hydrated, and encourage the shedding process.

You should never pick or peel at your dragon's shedding skin. Doing this can damage the new skin under the shedding skin. The skin will fall off as and when it's ready.

However, you should watch the tip of the tail and the toes during a shed. These can be problem areas during a shed, and if the skin doesn't shed properly from these areas, it can restrict the blood flow which can kill off the tissue. You can encourage these areas to shed properly by bathing the dragon and keeping the skin hydrated.

The shedding process is generated by hormones and has the purpose of regenerating the skin. It can't be predicted, as it doesn't regularly happen to adult dragons. Bearded dragons starting to peel will show symptoms such as a loss of appetite, pooping less, their skin colour turning a bit gray, and they simply don't want to be handled or touched anymore. One of the first places where they start shedding is around their eyes.

During this period, bearded dragons will start scratching with their legs and will rub their bodies on the floor, branches, or rocks in their tank. They will choose to spend more time away from the hot zone and will look for more humidity. A water source where they could just get wet could be helpful. Some owners even take warm baths to their dragons while shedding, but it depends on how much the pet can bear to be handled.

Humidity in the tank shouldn't get over the normal limit of 40 to 60%. The UVB light level should also be checked, as this is a very important part in the process. Owners mustn't peel off the old skin, as this is not helping the pet, but can damage the new skin.

Bearded dragons eat their old skin. Some say it is just a habit taken from the wild that helps them to keep predators away by removing traces of their scent. It could also be a sign that the pet needs more calcium in its diet.

During shedding, old skin and scales are replaced by new ones. It can last from several days to a few weeks. Your Dragon will seem more depressed or irritable during this period, so it would be best for you to leave him alone and show some support. What's most important is allowing him to shed by himself. There is a high risk of damaging the new skin if you try to peel or rip off the old one.

A week after week shower can help with the loosing of any shedding skin or you can utilize a splash jug to fog him with warm water, taking care that he doesn't chill after you fog him. Beardies likewise acknowledge something unpleasant to rub against amid the shedding process, so furnish him with an expansive, harsh stone or a bark—covered log for this reason. Be mindful so as not to hurt him in the event that you choose to have a go at picking off any substantial sheets of skin. Shedding skin on a beardie is similar to peeling skin off of a man with an awful sunburn. It ought to fall off effectively, yet in the event that it doesn't, allow it to sit unbothered.

My Bearded Dragon Is Constantly in Hiding

Bearded dragons like having a place to hide, but don't let this become too much of a habit. Time away from natural light and heating will cause depression and encourage the bearded dragon to stay away from the light for even longer. If you notice this happening, simply take away the bearded dragon's hiding place for a while.

Socialization

When housed together in the same tank, Dragons usually tend to climb on each other's back in order to get closer to the UV source and bask freely. It's really cute to watch. It's also true conflicts often occur between Dragons that share the same tank, and you will receive a few tips on how to avoid that too.

It's a known fact that baby Dragons who grow up together tend to develop a kind of special bond and are less likely to fight over territory during their adulthood. However, no matter how peaceful Beardies can be, you can never rely on their ability to put their instincts aside.

Socially speaking, Bearded Dragons seem to enjoy human company even more. They are highly adaptable and easily attached to their owners. Unlike iguanas, they aren't solitary and love to be in the center of attention.

However, too much attention can sometimes be overwhelming, and that's when they choose to hide. It's natural, even people feel the need to be alone every now and then. The point is, if you give your Dragon your heart, he'll give you his!

Nail Trimming

When you take a gander at them, the nails of your hairy mythical serpent may appear to be long and delicate, so their quality may be fairly shocking. They're extremely adaptable as well, and being so solid, they are exceptionally equipped for drawing blood when a beardie unleashes them on uncovered skin.

Out in the wild, a whiskery winged serpent gets a ton of activity. He is continually strolling crosswise over desert sand and shakes, moving up bushes or burrowing. The majority of that movement wears out his nails all the time, however in bondage, he most likely doesn't get such a great amount of chance to keep running about. Subsequent to beardie nails develop at an exceptionally quick rate, week by week trimming for your pet turns into a need.

On the off chance that you can discover them, then nail trimmers made particularly for reptiles will work exceptionally well for this reason. Feline nail trimmers make a decent substitute. You ought to additionally have a substance known as styptic powder prepared and holding up adjacent. This is a clean thickening specialists utilized by numerous veterinarians and pet groomers, who regularly buy them in the types of pencils to apply to the nails of canines and felines on the off chance that they've been trimmed too far.

At the point when a nail has been trimmed down excessively, you risk cutting the snappy. The snappy is a nervous wreck and veins that keeps running down the focal point of every nail. It's extremely delicate, as touchy as the brisk is in human nails, and if the nail is chopped down too far to harm it, the beardie is prone to snap his leg away in response. On the off chance that that happens, don't attempt to clutch him. Release him. In the event that you attempt to battle with him and hang on in any case, you chance harming his toes, his foot or his leg. Give him a few moments to quiet down, and investigate the nail for any harm. On the off chance that there's dying, simply plunge the toe into styptic powder and let it set for a couple of minutes before keeping on section whatever remains of his nails.

The most ideal approach to begin the section procedure is to let your beardie have a shower first. Run the water in the tub at around 80 degrees Fahrenheit and give him an opportunity to drench and unwind. Be watchful that it's not very hot with the goal that it blazes or overheats him, and be cautious that it's not very chilly so he becomes excessively slow, making it impossible to get out and move around. It additionally serves to set out a couple clothes at the base for your beardie to clutch, giving him grasp and keeping him from slipping around on a smooth, wet surface.

When he's casual and the nails have diminished up a little from absorbing the water, lift him up tenderly and lay him on your lap. Don't really attempt to snatch his foot or his toenail like you would with a youngster or a feline. That will just make them snap and battling, and you can hazard harming his toes. Simply reach over with the scissors, touching just the nail itself, and afterward cut.

Whenever trimming, simply remove the tip of every nail. There's no compelling reason to take off all that much. First and foremost, the delicate snappy is longer in reptiles than it is in warm blooded animals, and for another, your beardie needs his nails for moving about on things in his confine, particularly his luxuriating shake or roost.

Even if you have plenty of rocks within your vivarium (which can help to wear down the toe-nails) you will probably still need to clip your bearded dragon's toe nails every now and then.

Toe-nails can be clipped with nail clippers, although you have to be delicate. If you don't feel like doing it, you can of course take your beardie to the vets.

Keeping More Than One Bearded Dragon

Mixing more than one beardie is a careful balancing act. It's important to know what combinations of bearded dragons work well (and don't work well) together.

Two bearded dragons can live together in harmony but remember this isn't always the case. Males and females tend to get along better than males and males and females and females get along best.

In general, bearded dragons are quite sociable and having a friend is often welcomed, however bearded dragons can also be quite lonely creatures. Humans and bearded dragons work well together because humans are often away for chunks of the day, giving the beardie some space to himself for a few hours.

If you are going to keep more than one, two females work best but failing that a male and female. You will need to separate them when the male reaches sexual maturity (at around 12 months) as males can get quite aggressive at this time. Avoid putting a male and female from the same clutch together as for genetic reasons, this can cause a lot of health problems.

Males and males

Bearded dragons sometimes nip at the tails and feet of other bearded dragons, especially those younger or smaller. If you see this happening, there are two reasons for this that you should investigate. The first is simply because the bearded dragons are hungry and aren't being fed enough. The second is a sign of dominance.

If you do notice this happening make sure you're feeding your bearded dragons properly. If it is a case of dominance as opposed to feeding, you may need to consider getting a second vivarium or finding a new home for one of the bearded dragons if you do not have the resources and space for more than one vivarium.

There have been some cases where two male bearded dragons have managed to live together in harmony; however this is more often the exception rather than the rule.

Note: Usually the bearded dragons will circle each other before engaging in tail biting.

Remember, once you add a female to the vivarium, any 'bros before hoes' mentality gets thrown out the window and the two males are likely to start fighting each other, often viciously.

You can keep males on their own and even females on their own, although as mentioned before, beardies are quite solitary creatures and often your company is enough for them. Disease-wise this is also safer and mixing beardies can cause infections to spread if one of them gets sick, quickly doubling your problems.

Be aware that sexually mature males will try to mate with the female all of the time and some breeding experts recommend only allowing bearded dragons to mate once per year. On the mating note, avoid putting male and female siblings in the same vivarium. A bearded dragon can quickly get used to having you as a friend and for this reason you may not need a second or a third beardie.

Females and Females

This usually tends to work well, and can even work well with one male and many females although you will have to keep an eye on things just in case. An important consideration with all dragons, male and female, is their size in comparison to one another. If you have one bearded dragon that's larger than the other, that one is likely to assume a dominant role – this is the case of female/female communes as well as male/male. The more dominant bearded dragon is likely to eat first, occupy the prime basking areas and in some cases can be quite aggressive as well (although this isn't as big a problem with female/female communes as it is with male/male communes). It's just something to watch out for in case you find one of your bearded dragons isn't getting enough food or basking time.

There's no way you can't love these creatures, and if you have the space, time and wish to care for more Dragons, feel free to do it! But before you start planning, there are a few things you need to know.

If housed in the same tank

Bearded dragons are very territorial, so you have to make sure the tank is big enough for all of them. A larger tank will decrease the chances of conflict, although it is best to keep an eye on them at all times. There is a pretty low chance they might get along perfectly, and you always have to be prepared to separate them at the first sign of conflict or aggressive behavior.

Dragons of different ages

Adults can sometimes see hatchlings or juveniles as appetizers! Moreover, hatchlings are far too young for substrate, and this is a second reason to separate them until the baby grows old enough. If hatchlings and juveniles are stressed, they might end up refusing to eat, which will eventually lead to serious nutritional deficiencies and even death.

Hatchlings and juveniles need more care, and their food menu is the opposite of an adult Dragon's meal plan. They need to learn everything gradually, so you shouldn't expose them to the danger of being attacked by an older fellow. It's not fair competition, and you will have a hard time caring for them yourself.

Dragon Eggs!

A female Dragon can lay up to 20 eggs. However, she will instinctively eat the hatchlings if she makes eye contact with them. So those babies will have to learn how to live on their own, from the first day they spend in the outside world. And as long as they have enough insects and veggies, they'll manage!

Competition

It's a mistake to believe Bearded Dragons can't be competitive or aggressive. Competition may arise from several causes. One of them is space. Beardies can fight for the food bowl, basking space and even hiding places. If you decide to house two or more dragons in the same tank, make sure you provide additional caves and decorations for them to use.

Bearded Dragons also fight for females. Someone has to impress, and the best way to impress a female is expressing domination, proving that you deserve attention. In their attempt to dominate, dragons adopt an aggressive attitude and might end up attacking others, irrespective of the level of submission they show.

Prevent fights

There are a few ways to avoid conflict, and fortunately, not all of them are out of your hands. First of all, you can try housing males and females into separate tanks. Make sure tanks are big enough for all of them. Provide enough substrate, plastic plants, food bowls and hiding places for all of them. If they all have their own space, they won't feel invaded, and the risk of conflict is minimized.

Quarantine Periods

It's recommended that you put any new bearded dragons through a quarantine period, before mixing it with your current bearded dragon(s). This can help you spot any illnesses it has, or any behavioural problems before putting it into contact with any of the other (hopefully) healthy bearded dragons that you own.

Gestures

It will be so much fun watching these gestures, but you will definitely have a blast if you also know what they mean!

Head bobbing

Head bobbing is common during breeding seasons. It is performed by males wanting to show off in front of females and express domination. Let's assume that, in captivity a female is temporarily removed from the tank where she had been living with the male performing the gesture. When she will be brought back, that particular male will "welcome" her with the same head bobbing gesture, as if he would say something like "Watcha doin', hun?".

Arm waving

This gesture is specific to more submissive Dragons, often in response to head bobbing. It is one way of recognizing one's dominance and letting him know no one will cause any trouble. Some Beardies will even slightly bow down in sign of submission.

Eye bulging

Don't be scared – this is what your Dragon does when he feels he's got something in his eye. This is also common during shedding. No matter how weird it would look, the eyeball that's almost popping out of its socket is natural.

Beard display

When a Dragon "puffs out" its beard it can only mean two things. One, he's just showing off in front of the girls, hoping to intimidate competition and go up the hierarchy during the breeding season, or two, he's really, really angry.

Raised tail

During the breeding season, a raised tail is a sign of acceptance. It is also common in young Dragons stalking their prey.

Chapter 4: Feeding Your Bearded dragon

Water

Despite the fact that beardies originate from a desert atmosphere, regardless they require water each day. It makes up around two—thirds of their body weight. It keeps their body capacities general, and it's required for breath, processing, digestion system, waste disposal and then some. To put it plainly, beardies need water generally as each other living thing does. Furthermore, since they lose water each day through breath and poop, it should be supplanted. In spite of the fact that beardies will get water from some of their sustenance, particularly crisp leafy foods, they will at present need to drink with a specific end goal to take in enough.

Some beardies will drink out of a level, shallow dish, which ought to be kept low with the goal that they can without much of a stretch achieve it. This will purge out rapidly, so you should clean and refill it frequently. Some beardies likewise have a propensity for disposing of in their water – look out for this and make certain to keep their water clean.

You might procure a beardie who doesn't perceive a dish as a wellspring of water. Out in the wild, bowls are genuinely rare, all things considered. On the off chance that that is the situation, you might take a stab at filling the dish before him and letting him watch; after a few such exhibitions he might figure out how to compare the dish with water. You may likewise take a stab at adding a little organic product juice to the water to give it an inviting flavor.

A few proprietors give their beardies water through a splash jug that imitates how they would procure it in nature. In the event that you fog the body of your beardie, particularly along his back, you'll see that he will ordinarily level his body and afterward fix his back legs, which causes the beads of water to summary to his head. There, he can lick the water off of his nose and get a beverage. Beardies in the wild utilize the same procedure to extinguish their thirst with the morning dew.

Size of insects

Your dragon can't eat anything that is bigger than the area between the eyes of or the dragon. If you measure that area it will work as a handy measurement to have, when deciding what insects to buy. These come in various sizes from pinhead (which is about the size of an ant) to one-inch crickets.

The diet of a bearded dragon varies according to age:

Baby bearded dragon: 8-12 bugs and 1 salad daily (made up of approved vegetables)

1-year-old and older: 5-10 bugs a day plus a daily salad.

Remember that older bearded dragons are less active and thus need less food. The types of foods that should be included in the feeds are as follows:

• Crickets

• Dubai Roaches

• Wax Worms

• Phoenix Worms

• Hornworms

• Super worms

• Black soldier fly Larvae

• Locusts

You will find all the details of what's available for your bearded dragon by asking at your pet suppliers. You will also need to feed your insects so that they provide the best nutrition to your bearded dragon.

The salads can be made up from the following fruit and vegetables:

Fruit

The fruit below can be served to your bearded dragon, cut into small pieces, though do not offer your bearded dragon fruits not shown on this list, without first checking whether these are safe:

Apples, Apricots, Blackberries, Blueberries, Cherries, Cranberries, Figs, Grapes, Grapefruit, Mangos, Melons, Peaches, Nectarine, Papayas, Pears, Pineapple, Prunes, Strawberries, Watermelons, Raisins.

You need to remember the rule that a baby bearded dragon needs 80 percent bugs and 20 percent plants, while an adult needs the opposite, 80 percent plants and 20 percent bugs.

Rhubarb and Avocado are poisonous to your bearded dragon and should never be given.

Vitamins and supplements

Your bearded dragon may not have sufficient Vitamins supplied by the diet that you give him. It is therefore recommended that you purchase **Herptivite multivitamins**. Feeding your dragon a multivitamin will allow you to be sure about what vitamins your bearded dragon is eating, rather than risking under-or overdosing the bearded dragon on Vitamin A which could reach toxic levels.

Calcium and Vitamin D3 are also essential for your bearded dragon and this can be supplied by the use of **Rep-Cal Calcium Powder**. It should be used as follows:

Baby Dragons – A daily dose is required for bone formation.

Juvenile Dragons – this can be served with a meal 3-4 times a week.

Adult Dragons – Once a week with a meal

Green Plants

Vegetables that are permitted are shown here:

Acorn Squash, Artichoke Hearts, Raw Asparagus, Raw Bell Peppers, Bok Choy, Cabbage, Carrots, Celery, Chicory, Cucumbers, Collard Greens, Lentils, Endives, Kale, Raw Okra, Parsnips, Pumpkins, Turnip Greens, Yams, Raw Zucchini, Yellow Squash.

Do not feed your bearded dragon other vegetables without first checking to see if these are suitable as some vegetables can prove difficult for a bearded dragon, such as lettuce.

Zucchini, tomatoes and strawberries are all simple to develop and great decisions for a novice. Whatever you do, nonetheless, simply make sure that there are no pesticides or composts left on the nourishment – make sure to wash everything altogether.

You ought to additionally abstain from giving your beardie any sort of lettuce, particularly icy mass lettuce. There's no healthful worth in it, so it will essentially top him off without satisfying his dietary necessities. Lettuce ought to just be utilized to cajole a harmed or wiped out beardie to eat, since they do appear to appreciate it, however at no time ought to lettuce turn out to be a piece of his day by day diet.

Inserts, Worms and Other Live Foods

At the point when buying your bugs from a supplier, make certain to bolster them for no less than two days before offering them to your beardie. Most bugs don't eat when they're being sent or when they're kept in walled in areas at the pet shop, thus when you encourage these creepy crawlies to your beardie, he'll be getting an eager bug that has next to zero nutritious quality. Encouraging your creepy crawlies with profoundly nutritious nourishments before offering them to your reptile is a procedure called "gut stacking."

Notwithstanding the typical crickets, mealworms and waxworms, beardies appear to appreciate sowbugs, pillbugs, little child snails and once in a while a little night crawler. Simply watchful with the snails. The shells of littler snails are still delicate and can be passed, however the solidified shell of a grown-up can bring about impaction.

You ought to stay away from caterpillars, grasshoppers, moths and bugs since a large portion of these species are poisonous to a reptile. By no means if you ever give your beardie a firefly (otherwise called a lightning bug). These creepy crawlies contain phosphorous, which is exceedingly harmful to the beardie and can be deadly. Likewise maintain a strategic distance from any creepy crawlies with hard shells. These can't be processed and again could hazard impaction. Additionally ensure that the creepy crawlies you give your beardie aren't too extensive for him to process, regardless of what species they are. When in doubt, the bugs ought to be no bigger than the width between his eyes.

Crickets:

A standout amongst the most widely recognized creepy crawlies that can be given to reptiles is the cricket. For a long time these bugs have been trained and sustained to reptiles, creatures of land and water and fowls, which all appear to take pleasure in eating them. Odds are that in the event that you locate a pet shop offering any kind of reptile, will be offering feeder crickets. You can purchase them locally or you can purchase them in mass from mail request suppliers. They're additionally one of the simplest creepy crawlies to keep, raise and breed.

Keeping crickets until sustaining time is genuinely simple. Everything you need is a 10 to 20 gallon aquarium with a screen network spread, one that is secure and tight. These creepy crawlies will rapidly escape given a large portion of a shot. Put an inch or two of sand in the base, then include a few sticks, bark or paper egg containers for them to move over. You can give them water in a container top with a wipe settled within it. Never give them water sufficiently profound to suffocate in. Crickets inhale through spiracles in their thoraxes and guts, and if the crickets fall in and these ranges get to be submerged in water, they could suffocate on the off chance that they can't get retreat immediately. You can sustain the crickets anything remaining from the kitchen. Sustenance scraps are flawless, with the exception of meat and fat which go malodorous before long. Simply remember that whatever you bolster them is in the end going to go into your beardie. Make sure to drop in just a couple at once. Crickets can snack and nibble at your beardie, particularly around evening time when they're dynamic and he's resting. You don't need swarms of them in the enclosure.

Mealworms:

Mealworms are another most loved for pet shops to offer and reptile proprietors to purchase. While in the wild these are considered bugs, crushing grain supplies, and unshaven mythical beasts relish them and they're an extremely nutritious wellspring of nourishment. They're not any harder to raise than crickets. You can keep a bunch of mealworms in a 5 gallon tank with a screen network top, spread down some wheat or oat grain at the base, and keep them watered with a crisp cut of potato or yam set on top of the substrate. The worms will eat the vegetables and leave the skins, and their fecal matter is a sand—like substance. When you purchase mealworms, you're really purchasing the hatchlings of a creepy crawly known as Tenebrio molitor. On the off chance that left to develop, the mealworm will in the long run transform into a pupa and rise as a creepy crawly. Keep the tank temperature at around 75 to 80 degrees Fahrenheit to urge the mealworms to become quickly. Any cooler than that and their development will be hindered.

Mice

Pinky mice, which are newborn child, day—old mice who have not yet had their hide come in, can likewise be nourished to your beardie.

These are regularly given just as treats because of their high fat and protein content, particularly to female beardies why should about enter the reproducing season and start laying eggs.

Likewise with the bugs, your mice ought to be sustained a nutritious eating routine preceding bolstering them to your beardie. Youthful grown-up beardies can eat the pinky or infant mice, and full—grown grown-up beardies have been known not and eat youthful, little mice. Simply recall to bolster your beardie nothing that is bigger than the space between his eyes.

Vitamin Supplements

Managers frequently ask themselves for what valid reason they ought to give their beardies vitamin supplements on the off chance that they're giving a well—balanced diet, complete with an assortment of new vegetables and live creepy crawlies. Shouldn't he be getting all that he needs? Perhaps, however the issue is that you don't generally know where your beardie's nourishment originates from. Vegetables are just on a par with the dirt in which they were developed, and bugs are just comparable to the sustenance they're conveying in their gut. The same is valid for business reptile nourishment.

To ensure that your beardie is getting the best nourishment he can get, it's a smart thought to offer a youthful, quickly developing beardie a vitamin and mineral supplement arranged particularly for whiskery mythical serpents. You ought to give this supplement to adolescents around three to four times each week. Grown-ups will do fine when given a supplement around a few times each week. A large portion of these supplements are offered as powders which you tidy over the beardie's crickets seconds before encouraging time. Only place the bugs in a sack, hurl in some powder, then close it up and give it a tender shake to altogether coat the creepy crawlies before setting them down.

Important Note on Insect Storage

Sometimes these can be smelly and it is advised that you keep your storage container in a place outside of the home but the container should be portable so that you can take it into the garage on days when it is too cold or rainy. Do not forget to keep your insects fed so that they give the best nutritional value that they can to your bearded dragon.

It may sound complex, but when you get into the swing of feeding your bearded dragon, you will find that you will instinctively know when the best times to feed are and you will be able to balance their nutritional needs by keeping to the percentages shown above for live diet content and vegetable content.

Additional Feeding Guidelines: Insects & Worms

Fireflies look pretty, flying at night, but they're overall deadly for bearded dragons.

1. While it may be cute to imagine your bearded dragon chomping on some fireflies or lightning bugs, please don't do it. Fireflies are quite toxic to bearded dragons, and one good dose from a bunch of wild-caught fireflies from your backyard can actually kill your poor dragon.

2. Multivitamin and calcium supplementation is important for all pet lizards, not just bearded dragons. Supplements are administered through food dusting: a small amount of the chosen supplement is sprinkled on the food items prior to feeding. The lizard will naturally ingest the supplement once it starts feeding on the food that you gave.

3. Insects that are about 3/8 of an inch in size are recommended for juvenile bearded dragons. By 'juvenile' we refer specifically to dragons that are at least three months old.

4. Mealworms and other treats can be introduced when a bearded dragon is about four months old.

5. "Pinkies," or newborn mice, can be fed to reptiles, **but** they should be used sparingly.

As a treat you can give your adult bearded dragon ***one pinkie*** every seven days – that's the limit. I know that most beginning reptile keepers have a lot of fun feeding their pets but I do invite you to be more cautious.

Reptiles can learn to overfeed themselves if the owner feeds too frequently and, over time, this can actually shorten the reptile's lifespan.

Remember: it takes hours for a lizard to fully digest its food and detoxify its system. If you add too much food to a lizard's system, it places a lot of strain on the reptile's organs.

Additional pinkies can be given to an adult bearded dragon *if* (and only if) the beardie is heavy with eggs, or gravid. Gravid bearded dragons need additional protein and fat in their diet, so make sure to feed gravid beardies with lots of protein and, of course, their daily dose of supplements and greens. Baby mice should only be given once a week as a treat.

6. Hatchlings are generally more voracious than their older counterparts, so don't be concerned if the smaller lizards in your terrarium appear hungrier than the rest. Just feed your young dragons two to three times a day, and they should be fine.

7. *Gut loading* is very important step in the feeding process. While it is true that bearded dragons eat nongut loaded insects in the wild, it is also true that they only receive a limited amount of food every time

they are fed. So, in reality, bearded dragons may become undernourished if the insects they are being fed are not "full," or fed themselves.

You can solve this problem easily by feeding the prey items before they are, in turn, fed to your bearded dragon.

Many reptile enthusiasts feed their prey items with stuff such as mashed vegetables and even commercial baby food. What's important is that the crickets/worms/locusts that you are about to give your bearded dragon are well fed themselves.

The gut loading should be performed exactly twentyfour hours before the actual feeding. Having a regular feeding schedule will lessen the burden of having to gut load your prey items.

You can gut load prey items by batch. For example, if you feed your dragon at 9 AM, begin gut loading the first batch *for the next morning* immediately after feeding your pet.
 If the second feeding is around 2 PM, gut load the **second batch** for the next day's second feeding. Do this and feeding time will be very easy indeed.

8. While it is true that bearded dragons will happily munch on almost any kind of worm, try to feed your pet with worms that *have just molted.* Molting refers to the process of shedding skin or exoskeleton.

The exoskeleton of worms protects the fragile internal organs; as such, the exoskeleton is harder to digest. Over time, the chitin (exoskeleton) from worms can cause painful intestinal impactions.

9. In a previous section I shared with you a table of food ratios. Notice that fully-grown adults need less protein overall compared to younger dragons. The reason for this is quite simple: fully grown dragons no longer need large amounts of protein to ***grow.***

They just need to maintain their existing musculature, and the whole physiological accomplish that requires less remember: the older your bearded dragon, the more vegetables it should be consuming!

10. Gravid bearded dragons generally require more nutrients. We're talking about more vegetables, worms, insects, and pinkies. Females who are heavy with eggs also require ***more calcium supplementation.*** Multivitamin supplements should also be increased to two to four times ***per week.*** Non-gravid females and males only require once weekly multivitamin supplementation.

11. Ideally, larger worms should only be given to bearded dragons that have attained ***at least twelve inches*** in size.

Chapter 5: Breeding the Bearded dragon

This is a difficult, but interesting process experienced owners often turn to. It's not recommended if you are emotionally attached to your Dragons, since injury and death often occur in the process. As an interesting fact, after laying the eggs, the female leaves and lets them hatch alone. If a female sees eggs, she will eat them!

You need thorough documentation and many years of experience with all sorts of reptiles in order to become an experienced breeder. The breeder you got your Dragon from might be able help you with more information and guidance for you to start off!

Bearded dragons are relatively complicated to breed in comparison to many other household lizard species. The process will involve you owning a vivarium for each of your bearded dragons as well as a vivarium reserved for the mating process, an incubator and a laying box.

As previously mentioned sexing bearded dragons is a complicated process and it is recommended to have your lizards sexed by a professional vet before attempting breeding. It is also important to feed your female bearded dragon an increased about of gut loaded and nutrient rich food before initiating the breeding process. It is also best practice to feed your female lizard a supplement rich in vitamin D daily to help ensure that her eggs will be adequately calcified. You will need to prepare your male and female bearded dragon for brumation about two months before the breeding process to optimize their fertility.

Preparing the Breeding Habitat

Although your male and female bearded dragons should only be housed together temporarily it is important that the enclosure is set up for optimal breeding. Firstly the enclosure needs to be large enough to house two adult bearded dragons. Secondly the vivarium has to be set up in a manner similar to each individual bearded dragons regular housing to avoid stressing the lizards. It is best practice to provide a larger than normal flat basking stone to allow your lizards to breed.

The Breeding Process

Place your bearded dragons into the designated breeding enclosure. It will take a minimum of a few hours for your bearded dragons to start mating as they will need some time to adjust to their new surroundings and one another. Once the breeding process is completed you should wait around a week before placing each bearded dragon back into their respective vivarium. You should then keep them apart for one week and then place them back together again for another breeding session and to ensure that the breeding has been successful.

If the breeding process has been successful and your female bearded dragon has become pregnant she may start to pace around her enclosure and dig erratically. It is also not uncommon for pregnant beardies to eat less during their pregnancy. You should be able to visibly see the eggs within the females belly about four to six weeks after the mating process. When your bearded dragon exhibits this behavior it is best practice to gently move her to the designated lay box so she can lay her eggs. Once in the lay box your bearded dragon will begin digging to create an area to lay her eggs. Once the eggs have been laid it is best practice to quickly move your bearded dragon back

into their vivarium. Most females will lay around 24 eggs at a time –
but can also lay as few as 15 and as many as 50. If your bearded
dragon has been in the lay box for multiple days without laying eggs
she might be suffering with egg binding – if this is the case you should
take your bearded dragon to the vet IMMEDIATELY.

Incubation

Before the laying process it is best practice to prepare your incubator.
Make a small thumb impression in the perlite (which should come as
standard you're your incubator) which lines the incubator. After they
have been laid it is best practice to place the eggs in the incubator as
quickly as possible. Lift the eggs gently with your hand and place
them in the incubator in a similar orientation to how they were laid. It
may be helpful to mark the top of the egg with a pen to prevent you
accidently turning the egg upside down. Place one egg into one of the
previously made thumb impressions – the egg should fit snuggly.
Maintain the incubator temperature between 82 and 86 degrees
Fahrenheit. It is important to keep the correct temperature or the
embryos inside the egg will most likely die. It is best to follow your
individual incubators instruction when it comes to humidity levels as
each one is going to be different. It is best practice to check on the
eggs about twice a week as it is important to check that they eggs do
not have condescension or are overly dry – as both can cause harm to
the embryo. Healthy and fertile eggs will increase to about twice their

original size and turn a chalky white. Unfertile eggs will turn a pinkish or greenish color.

Bearded dragon eggs take between 60 to 70 days to hatch. At around the 60 day mark the eggs may begin to dimple and produce water droplets – do not worry as this is completely normal and indicates that the eggs will be hatching soon. There may also be a slit running the length of the egg which is likewise normal and is created by the baby bearded dragons 'egg tooth' on their snout. It is important to allow the baby bearded dragons to emerge from their eggs on their own which typically takes around 24 to 36 hours. You should keep the newly born bearded dragons in their incubator for the first 24 hours of their life. Sadly during each hatching it is not uncommon for some of the baby dragons to die – if this is the case it is best practice to remove deceased hatchlings are quickly as possible. After they have all hatched you should group the babies together into small tanks (for example 20 gallons) depending on their size. You will not need to feed the hatchlings for the first three days as they are able to survive on the yolk from their eggs. After three days it is important to start providing the babies with a lot of food to help them grow – at this stage it is imperative to remove any dominant bearded dragons to allow the smaller ones to eat as well.

Chapter 6: Keeping Your Bearded dragon Healthy

Bearded dragons are generally very robust and hardy lizards which are great assets when you are new to lizard keeping. The initial few days and weeks can be very stressful to both pet and owner but knowing that you already have a study and strong lizard can remove a lot of unnecessary fretting and worrying.

Keeping your dragon healthy is very important. We've talked about finding a reptile veterinarian, but you should know the signs of some of the most common bearded dragons illnesses, and what your dragon should look like when he's healthy.

There are times when your healthy bearded dragon can seem ill, but it may be because he is shedding or brumating.

Great wellbeing happens from a spotless confine, legitimate nourishment and consideration amid taking care of. Once in a while, your beardie will become ill without anybody being at shortcoming. It's essential to know the side effects of the different issue and maladies, and it's critical to comprehend what to do when such circumstances crop up.

Finding a Good Veterinarian

Most veterinarians are not appropriately prepared to handle the one of a kind needs of the more extraordinary pets, particularly reptiles. These are altogether different creatures to mutts and felines, requiring distinctive medicines and hardware, and they are frequently more sensitive and troublesome patients. Consequently, not all veterinarians will to see a whiskery mythical beast, so you might need to do some footwork to discover one.

Before you even procure your unshaven mythical beast, you ought to discover a veterinarian for him. It will benefit neither you nor the beardie in any way to be hunting down a gifted vet subsequent to something has turned out badly when there might be a crisis circumstance. In the event that you need to take him to the primary veterinarian you can discover, you might be getting treatment that isn't as talented as the beardie needs.

To discover a veterinarian who will treat reptiles, you can search for Yellow Pages notices in the telephone directory. Numerous will publicize their readiness to acknowledge reptiles as an offering point for individuals simply like you. You can likewise talk with any companions in the zone who own reptiles and get a referral from them. Nearby herpetological clubs will likewise have postings of respectable veterinarians. The Association of Reptilian and Amphibian Veterinarians is a gathering of vets who have an enthusiasm for or have practical experience in reptiles. You can take a stab at keeping in touch with them for proposals of good veterinarians in your general vicinity.

When you do have the names of a couple vets in your general vicinity who'll treat hairy winged serpents, make meetings with a few of them. Be arranged to pay for the workplace visits and make a rundown of things to ask with you before you go. Pay consideration on how the veterinarian answers these inquiries, how he or she treats you and your creature, and how promising, mindful and instructed he or she is. This is the individual upon whom you'll need to depend when things turn out badly. Ensure you're exceptionally alright with the decision before turning into a customer.

A few inquiries you will need to ask are:

- Have you by and by possessed reptiles?
- Do you see numerous unshaven mythical beasts as patients? Have you effectively treated numerous beardies?
- Is your office staff prepared to handle and watch over reptiles?
- Do you have warmed confines for reptiles who are experiencing therapeutic methodology?
- Is it accurate to say that you are accessible twilight?
- Do you acknowledge charge cards or installment arranges?

These pets need at least one veterinarian visit every year for a regular check. All sudden changes in a bearded dragon's behaviour, like depression, lost appetite, lethargy can be non-specific symptoms and require a veterinarian evaluation.

Early diagnosis pays dividends.

Is your dragon listless and/or lethargic?

Is your dragon eating as well as per normal?

Is your dragon looking dull, off color?

What you must realize and you will gain the knowledge by experience, is that a dragon can take on all of these appearances when it is about to shed the skin.

If you are not sure, do not be afraid to consult an expert such as your local veterinary surgeon, your local pet shop, your dragon breeder, the local herpetological society or a care center (zoo) that specializes in lizards, You will generally find that these outlets are staffed by people who have a common interest in all things reptile and lizard and they will gladly pass on any advice to you on any topic relating to your dragon.

Remember, knowledge is king.

Coccida

Bearded dragons have their very own nasty species of internal parasite of coccidium, Isospora amphiboluri. This is an insidious problem impairing the digestive system of your dragon and can be fatal. If your dragon is listless, lethargic and generally run down and has smelly, runny stools which tend to stick to the rear of your dragon, coccidian could be present. As with the other internal parasites seek immediate expert professional help.

Respiratory Ailments

It is generally caused by improper living conditions. Most common signs are sneezing, bubbles in the mouth, nasal or ocular discharge, and lethargy. Regular treatment is based on antibiotics, but some cases also require hospital care.

The risk of avoiding these problems can also be diminished by feeding and caring well for your dragon, as a happy contented healthy lizard will have less chance of falling prey to most ailments. A scrupulously clean habitat will also help towards the ongoing health of your dragon.

However, even dragons can experience problems in prolonged periods of cold and/or damp and poorly ventilated vivarium/terrarium.

A bad bout of internal parasites, Endoparasites can also exasperate respiratory problems. Respiratory ailments are very much in self evidence.

- Sneezing
- Rapid breathing
- Shallow breathing
- Rasping
- Bubbling around the mouth accompanying each breath
- Listless and lethargic
- Upon noticing any of these indicators of breathing problems, immediately seek professional expert advice and help.

Metabolic Bone Disease

In simple terms Metabolic Bone Disease is the lack of sufficient calcium and vitamin D3. Insufficient calcium from the diet and not enough vitamin D3 from either direct sunlight, UVA/UVB lighting or from a supplement.

D3 is the vitamin that enables the body to utilize calcium. When the level of blood calcium drops, the parathyroid glands then begin extracting calcium from the bones and redistributing it to the bloodstream.

Symptoms include:

- Convulsions
- Twitching of limbs
- Swollen limbs and very often pliable
- Soft jawbones
- Chubby face

Once again it is imperative to seek expert help if you notice any of these symptoms because in the early stages, this malady is treatable.

Which is generally caused by a bad diet, too rich in Phosphorus and low in calcium and Vitamin D3. The main signs of the disease are swelling of the mandible, softening of the facial bones, and/or swelling of the hind legs and toes. Generally it is common for young dragons. It can be treated with calcium, multi-vitamin or mineral supplements. UVB light is very important in preventing and treating this disorder.

Infectious stomatitis (mouth rot)

Which is a bacterial condition that causes pinpoint haemorrhages on the gums, an excess amount of mucus, ulcers and losing teeth. It can be caused not only by viruses and bacteria, but also by trauma or poor nutrition. The right treatment is done with antibiotics.

Parasites

The most common being mites, ticks, and pinworms. Internal parasites are generally identified after the microscopic fecal examination (should be done at least once a year), and treatment will be provided by the veterinarian according to the results. For mites and ticks, there are also good treatments that can be prescribed by the vet.

Parasites (External)

Ectoparasites are external parasites and are easier to diagnose and to treat than the internal variety. Ticks and mites are quite easy to see and they can be 'dusted' with a propriety powder that you can obtain from your local pet shop or breeder. Read and follow the instructions as per the product and all should be fine. Just a gentle word of warning, be a little more careful with hatchlings or young dragons and if you feel unsure always seek advice from your pet shop or veterinarian.

Parasites (Internal)

Endoparasites are internal parasites and are by their nature more difficult for the general layperson to diagnose.

It is taken for granted that that in the wild natural habitat, dragons will have parasites, both internal and external, but it is not so well known that even captive bred dragons can harbor Endoparasites and also some other pathogens.

The most common of internal parasites are:

- Tapeworms
- Pinworms
- Roundworms
- Nematodes

You can normally diagnose these parasites by fecal (faeces-stool) examination.

Seek advice from your veterinarian who will decide whether your dragon needs treatment or not.

This is a specialist treatment and involves administering a substance that could be fatal to your dragon if given in the wrong dosages. Let your trained reptile expert do work and calculations for you.

The major part that you can play if your dragon is exhibiting signs of infestation is to keep the home of your dragon scrupulously clean and tidy. Parasitic problems and reinfestation can be prevented by this one simple task.

Hypervitaminosis D

It is caused by too many vitamin supplements given to the pet or by feeding it dog or cat food. This is one of the most difficult conditions in dragons and normally the pet should be hospitalized. Diet will have to be changed in this case.

Many bearded dragons carry **salmonella** in their system. This doesn't make them sick, but can harm their owners. To avoid salmonella infections, owners should always wash their hands with soap and water after touching their pets. Always watch children in the presence of the reptiles, and never bathe the bearded dragon in the sink or the bathtub.

Stress

Albeit hairy mythical beasts are, by nature, quiet and delicate of demeanor, they can be maddened or annoyed with specific things. At the point when this happens continually, it can bring about a negative response in the resistant framework. Focused on beardies are more inclined to becoming ill, can quit eating or in the end simply pass on. It's imperative to watch out for your beardie and watch out for any indications of anxiety, then be prepared to bail him out and quiet him down.

Some conceivable reasons for anxiety are:

The wrong enclosure: Hatchlings can live in genuinely little confines, yet a bigger beardie needs space to move around. A confine too little for your reptile will push him, and he'll respond by tossing himself against the dividers.

The wrong environment: Air that is excessively cool or excessively muggy can harm your beardie's wellbeing. He won't have the capacity to process appropriately, might get respiratory diseases, and he'll neglect to flourish.

Mirrors: Males are exceptionally regional creatures, and in the event that they see themselves in a mirror, they might attempt to battle their own appearance. Make a point to bring down or move any mirrors in which he may see himself.

Endoparasites:

Not just can your beardie be beset with clutters that come to fruition from poor sustenance and injury, yet he can likewise be tormented by interior parasites. Frequently, these are much harder to identify than outside parasites, so a normal checkup with the veterinarian is basic to great wellbeing. A fecal examination can uncover the vicinity of parasites, and veterinarians search for bodily fluid or blood in the stool and any obvious worms. Any adjustment in hankering, lost life or more regular poops can likewise be side effects, so make sure to tell the vet on the off chance that you see any of these.

Impactions

At the point when a beardie ingests a lot of a substance that he can't process, his framework might get to be blocked. This is called impaction. It is possibly deadly, and its manifestations incorporate bloating and spewing. On the off chance that you trust your beardie has gotten to be affected, don't defer in getting him to a veterinarian. Surgery might be required to spare his life.

Impaction can be forestalled by giving your beardie sustenance that is no bigger than the space between his eyes and by giving him a suitable substrate.

Nourishing Disorders

A malnourished beardie is a dismal sight. He will look got dried out, his skin will seem wrinkled, the bones will be noticeable and the eyes will be indented. He is additionally at a high hazard for an assortment of disarranges that might assault his debilitated body and safe framework, particularly an especially terrible one called Metabolic Bone Disease.

MBD's side effects incorporate the accompanying: anorexia, dying, obstruction, gingivitis, mouth decay, an inability to flourish, bend of the spine, seizures and tremors, swelling in the appendages, broken or diminished bones, and kidney issues. It's brought about when the beardie is not getting enough calcium, and his body starts to take it from his unresolved issues the inadequacy. Calcium is required for the blood, heart capacities, muscle capacity and the digestion system of nourishment, so it must be given in adequate amounts to keep these side effects.

Treatment starts by rectifying the eating regimen. Include more vegetables that are high in calcium such as collard greens, turnip greens, mustard and kale. UVB lighting ought to be given, and if conceivable, take your beardie out into the daylight. A few veterinarians may treat MBD with infusions of calcium, vitamin D3 and calcitonin. Oral neocalglucon might likewise be recommended. Wholesome clutters are best counteracted instead of treated.

Smolder Wounds and Trauma

Notwithstanding your each push to be sheltered, mischances can happen. In the event that something happens that outcomes in your beardie being harmed, the most essential thing to do is to resist the urge to panic. Your frenzy can agitate your beardie, which can irritate his condition further.

You might need to control your beardie, and in the event that he's pushed from the reason for his harm, he won't be helpful. At this moment, he's particularly powerless against predators, and his impulses are going to instruct him to run and stow away. He might thrash and whip his tail when you endeavor to lift him up, and you will need to control his tail to counteract him harming himself further. You can likewise attempt to cover his head with a towel to quiet him, however this doesn't work with all beardies. Wrap his body with a washcloth or a towel to keep yourself from getting pricked by his spines, and hold his legs collapsed back along his body. You just need to uncover the harmed range.

Injury can be intense. In the event that your beardie gives off an impression of being stifling or choking, open his mouth and examine. There is no Heimlich move for beardies, so on the off chance that you can't uproot the deterrent with a couple of tweezers, you have to surge him to the veterinarian as fast as would be prudent.

Draining comes in a few structures. The first is seeping underneath the skin, bringing about wounding or a hematoma. Wounding itself is not genuine, but rather a veterinarian will need to see to a hematoma. At the main indication of seeping underneath the skin, put a little ice pack on the influenced zone for only a few moments at once to cool the territory without cooling your beardie. In the event that it proceeds with, contact your veterinarian at the earliest opportunity. The second is an outside consistent overflowing, and this is more genuine. Place weight and dressing on the injury to staunch it, then get your beardie to the vet before he seeps to death. In the event that the draining comes in spurts, this is even genuine still. You can make a tourniquet out of a shoelace or cloth wrap to tie around an appendage or a tail, being mindful so as to attach it sufficiently tight to moderate the draining however not break bones. Each ten to fifteen minutes, slacken the tourniquet to give the tissue a chance to receive some blood stream. The third shape, interior dying, is hard to recognize and greatly perilous. On the off chance that your beardie has taken a fall, watch his conduct for some time. In the event that he develops drowsy, quits moving, inhales through his mouth or has grisly stool, regurgitation or spit, then get him to the veterinarian straight away.

Smolders can occur from getting excessively near a glowing light or a warmth source. Prompt veterinary consideration is expected to treat this. Get a little ice pack and over and again put this on and off the blaze while you are en route to the vet's office. Put it on to cool the smolder, however take it off so that your beardie doesn't take a lot of a chill.

Protection Medicine

Keeping up your beardie's general wellbeing is the best technique for keeping any major issues. Legitimate nourishment, cleanliness and a suitable situation will all guarantee that your beardie stays cheerful and solid for a long time.

Cleanliness implies customary tending to the enclosures and lessening the dangers of cross—contamination. You can keep the transmission of maladies by:

Keeping enclosures and furniture clean.

Disposing of defecation in a shut rubbish sack. Try not to add them to a fertilizer pile.

Never washing your beardie's enclosure, furniture or nourishment dishes in the kitchen. Use separate instruments for the employment and go outside, into a cellar or an extra restroom.

Using a solid bleachand—water answer for sanitize everything once perfect.

Never kissing your beardie; this could contaminate you or the reptile.

Zoonoses

Microorganisms which can be transmitted from creatures to people and the other way around are known as zoonoses or zoonotic maladies. Salmonella is a standout amongst the most well-known ones, and shockingly it's a standout amongst the most widely recognized and typical intestinal microorganisms found in reptiles. There's no verification that every single hairy monster convey salmonella, however numerous do.

These can be hazardous to individuals who are immunocompromised because of illnesses, for example, HIV, being taking drugs, or from different medicines they are accepting. Kids under 8 years of age are likewise more prone to experience the ill effects of zoonotic disease than grown-ups, so they ought to be directed nearly while in contact with the reptile. Pregnant moms should likewise be amazingly cautious in their treatment of anything to do with the reptiles, as hatchlings are additionally at awesome danger. For them, it might be best to simply leave the cleaning errands to another person.

Zoonosesare totally preventable by great cleanliness practices, for example, keeping all enclosure hardware spotless and intensive hand—washing in the wake of taking care of your beardie. With a tad bit of consideration and consideration, there's no motivation behind why anybody shouldn't have the capacity to appreciate the organization of a hairy monster.

Constipation

Constipation can be a common illness with bearded dragons and it should be obvious when this is happening.

One of the most common causes for constipation is low temperatures as this can prevent the bearded dragon from being able to digest properly. Make sure your temperatures are set to those recommended within the heating and lighting chapter.

Routine Vet Visits

It's important to take your bearded dragon to the vet for a checkup every now and then, as you would with a dog, cat or even with a human. There are a number of parasites, both internal and external, that bearded dragons are prone to and regular checkups with your vet are recommended.

Conclusion

Keeping bearded dragons as pets is a relatively new trend, but one that is rapidly growing and evolving. As a related trend, bearded dragon experts are now popping up everywhere; which is both a good and a bad thing. More information and people sharing their own experiences is obviously a positive but caution and research are essential when doing homework online, for anything really, not just bearded dragons.

Although personality is definitely a key factor, another reason bearded dragons have become so sought after is due to the fact that it is very easy to keep them as pets. Unlike cats or dogs, beardies don't need much space, and even when compared to other reptiles such as snakes and iguanas their needs are relately straight-forward.

Being easy to look after, bearded dragons are naturally a popular pet for children. Having a lot of personality and charisma also helps as it means children are less likely to get bored with them, which with others pets can leave mummy and daddy with a few unexpected chores.

Your dragon requires only occasional feeding no long walks and you do not have to keep it amused for hours on end. But what it will require, as all responsible pet owners realize, is love, attention and dedication to the wellbeing and care of the beautiful bearded dragon.

With the right diet, housing and care, most bearded dragons just 'get on with it'. If you follow some basic advice, there are generally few problems or behavioral issues to worry about.

If something does go wrong, most vets will have at least a basic understanding of reptiles and should be able to treat your bearded dragon. Your pet shop owner or local vet should be able to give you more information on this, but failing that you can ask on one of the many reptile forums that exist online.

Made in the USA
Coppell, TX
18 November 2021

65986815R00057